CLASSIC VANILLA CHIA SEED PUDDING	2
CHOCOLATE BLISS CHIA DELIGHT	4
BERRY BURST CHIA PARFAIT	6
MANGO TANGO CHIA FUSION	8
COCONUT CREAM PIE CHIA INDULGENCE	10
ALMOND JOY CHIA DREAM	12
PUMPKIN SPICE CHIA HARVEST	14
MATCHA GREEN TEA CHIA ZEN	16
SALTED CARAMEL CHIA DELIGHT	18
ESPRESSO HAZELNUT CHIA EUPHORIA	20
POMEGRANATE PASSION CHIA BLISS	22
LEMON RASPBERRY CHIA SYMPHONY	24
MAPLE WALNUT CHIA SYMPHONY	26
BLUEBERRY LEMON CHEESECAKE CHIA EXTRAVAGANZA	28
PEANUT BUTTER BANANA CHIA HEAVEN	31
TIRAMISU TOFFEE CHIA TEMPTATION	33
PISTACHIO ROSEWATER CHIA SERENITY	35
ORANGE CREAMSICLE CHIA FANTASY	37
STRAWBERRY SHORTCAKE CHIA ROMANCE	39
CHAI SPICED CHIA LATTE LOVE	42
COOKIES AND CREAM CHIA FANTASY	45
CHERRY ALMOND CHIA JUBILEE	47
GINGERBREAD COOKIE CHIA JOY	49
CHOCOLATE RASPBERRY CHIA FANTASY	52
CINNAMON ROLL CHIA DELIGHT	54
HAZELNUT HONEY CHIA HARMONY	56
KIWI LIME CHIA ZEST	58
SNICKERDOODLE CHIA CELEBRATION	60
APPLE PIE CHIA EXTRAVAGANZA	62
LAVENDER BLUEBERRY CHIA SERENADE	64

Classic Vanilla Chia Seed Pudding

Ingredients:

- 1/4 cup chia seeds
- 1 cup milk (almond milk, coconut milk, or any milk of your choice)
- 1-2 tablespoons maple syrup or honey (adjust to taste)
- 1/2 teaspoon vanilla extract

Instructions:

1. In a mixing bowl, combine the chia seeds, milk, maple syrup (or honey), and vanilla extract.
2. Whisk everything together until well combined.
3. Cover the bowl with plastic wrap or a lid and refrigerate for at least 2 hours, or overnight. This allows the chia seeds to absorb the liquid and thicken.
4. After the pudding has set, give it a good stir to break up any clumps and evenly distribute the chia seeds.
5. Divide the pudding into serving cups or bowls.
6. Optional: Top with your favorite fruits, nuts, or a sprinkle of cinnamon for extra flavor.

7. Enjoy your delicious and nutritious Vanilla Chia Seed Pudding!

Notes:

- This pudding can be stored in the refrigerator for up to 5 days, making it a great meal prep option.
- Feel free to adjust the sweetness to your liking by adding more or less maple syrup or honey.
- Experiment with different toppings such as fresh berries, sliced bananas, shredded coconut, or chopped nuts.

Chocolate Bliss Chia Delight

Ingredients:

- 1/4 cup chia seeds
- 1 cup milk (almond milk, coconut milk, or any milk of your choice)
- 2 tablespoons cocoa powder
- 2-3 tablespoons maple syrup or honey (adjust to taste)
- 1/2 teaspoon vanilla extract
- A pinch of salt
- Optional toppings: sliced bananas, berries, shredded coconut, chopped nuts

Instructions:

1. In a mixing bowl, combine the chia seeds, milk, cocoa powder, maple syrup (or honey), vanilla extract, and a pinch of salt.
2. Whisk everything together until the cocoa powder is fully incorporated and there are no lumps.
3. Cover the bowl with plastic wrap or a lid and refrigerate for at least 2 hours, or overnight. This allows the chia seeds to absorb the liquid and thicken.

4. After the pudding has set, give it a good stir to break up any clumps and evenly distribute the chia seeds and cocoa.
5. Divide the chocolate chia pudding into serving cups or bowls.
6. Optional: Top with sliced bananas, berries, shredded coconut, or chopped nuts for added flavor and texture.
7. Enjoy your indulgent Chocolate Bliss Chia Delight!

Notes:

- This pudding can be stored in the refrigerator for up to 5 days.
- Adjust the sweetness to your liking by adding more or less maple syrup or honey.
- For a thicker pudding, use less milk. For a thinner consistency, add more milk.
- Experiment with different toppings to create your favorite chocolate chia pudding variation.

Berry Burst Chia Parfait

Ingredients:

- 1/4 cup chia seeds
- 1 cup milk (almond milk, coconut milk, or any milk of your choice)
- 2 tablespoons maple syrup or honey (adjust to taste)
- 1/2 teaspoon vanilla extract
- 1 cup mixed berries (strawberries, blueberries, raspberries)
- 1/2 cup granola
- Optional: Greek yogurt or coconut yogurt

Instructions:

1. In a mixing bowl, combine the chia seeds, milk, maple syrup (or honey), and vanilla extract.
2. Whisk everything together until well combined.
3. Cover the bowl with plastic wrap or a lid and refrigerate for at least 2 hours, or overnight. This allows the chia seeds to absorb the liquid and thicken.
4. After the pudding has set, give it a good stir to break up any clumps and evenly distribute the chia seeds.

5. In serving glasses or bowls, layer the chia pudding with mixed berries and granola.
6. Repeat the layers until you reach the top of the glass, ending with a layer of berries and granola on top.
7. Optional: Add a dollop of Greek yogurt or coconut yogurt between the layers for extra creaminess.
8. Chill in the refrigerator for at least 30 minutes before serving.
9. Enjoy your refreshing and delicious Berry Burst Chia Parfait!

Notes:

- This parfait can be assembled ahead of time and stored in the refrigerator for up to 2 days.
- Feel free to customize with your favorite fruits and toppings.
- If you prefer a sweeter parfait, add more maple syrup or honey to the chia pudding.
- For a dairy-free option, use coconut yogurt instead of Greek yogurt.

Mango Tango Chia Fusion

Ingredients:

- 1/4 cup chia seeds
- 1 cup coconut milk
- 1 ripe mango, peeled and diced
- 2 tablespoons honey or agave syrup (adjust to taste)
- 1/2 teaspoon vanilla extract
- Optional toppings: sliced mango, shredded coconut, chopped nuts

Instructions:

1. In a blender, combine the diced mango, coconut milk, honey (or agave syrup), and vanilla extract.
2. Blend until smooth and creamy.
3. In a mixing bowl, combine the chia seeds and the mango coconut mixture.
4. Whisk everything together until well combined.
5. Cover the bowl with plastic wrap or a lid and refrigerate for at least 2 hours, or overnight. This allows the chia seeds to absorb the liquid and thicken.

6. After the pudding has set, give it a good stir to break up any clumps and evenly distribute the chia seeds and mango.
7. Divide the Mango Tango Chia Fusion into serving cups or bowls.
8. Optional: Top with sliced mango, shredded coconut, or chopped nuts for added flavor and texture.
9. Enjoy your tropical and refreshing Mango Tango Chia Fusion!

Notes:

- This pudding can be stored in the refrigerator for up to 5 days.
- Adjust the sweetness to your liking by adding more or less honey or agave syrup.
- Feel free to use other fruits such as pineapple or papaya for variations.
- If you prefer a smoother texture, you can blend the chia pudding again before serving.

Coconut Cream Pie Chia Indulgence

Ingredients:

- 1/4 cup chia seeds
- 1 cup coconut milk (full-fat for creamier texture)
- 2 tablespoons maple syrup or honey (adjust to taste)
- 1/2 teaspoon vanilla extract
- 1/4 cup shredded coconut (sweetened or unsweetened)
- 1/4 cup graham cracker crumbs
- Whipped cream or coconut whipped cream for topping (optional)

Instructions:

1. In a mixing bowl, combine the chia seeds, coconut milk, maple syrup (or honey), and vanilla extract.
2. Whisk everything together until well combined.
3. Add the shredded coconut and graham cracker crumbs to the mixture. Stir until evenly distributed.
4. Cover the bowl with plastic wrap or a lid and refrigerate for at least 2 hours, or overnight.

This allows the chia seeds to absorb the liquid and thicken.
5. After the pudding has set, give it a good stir to break up any clumps and ensure an even texture.
6. Divide the coconut chia pudding into serving cups or bowls.
7. Optional: Top each serving with a dollop of whipped cream or coconut whipped cream.
8. Sprinkle some additional shredded coconut or graham cracker crumbs on top for garnish, if desired.
9. Enjoy your delicious Coconut Cream Pie Chia Indulgence!

Notes:

- This pudding can be stored in the refrigerator for up to 5 days.
- For added coconut flavor, you can toast the shredded coconut before adding it to the pudding.
- If you prefer a sweeter pudding, adjust the amount of maple syrup or honey accordingly.
- Feel free to get creative with toppings like fresh berries or a sprinkle of cinnamon.

Almond Joy Chia Dream

Ingredients:

- 1/4 cup chia seeds
- 1 cup coconut milk (full-fat for creamier texture)
- 2 tablespoons cocoa powder
- 2-3 tablespoons maple syrup or honey (adjust to taste)
- 1/2 teaspoon almond extract
- 1/4 cup shredded coconut (sweetened or unsweetened)
- 2 tablespoons sliced almonds
- Optional: Dark chocolate chips for garnish

Instructions:

1. In a mixing bowl, combine the chia seeds, coconut milk, cocoa powder, maple syrup (or honey), and almond extract.
2. Whisk everything together until the cocoa powder is fully incorporated and there are no lumps.
3. Add the shredded coconut and sliced almonds to the mixture. Stir until evenly distributed.
4. Cover the bowl with plastic wrap or a lid and refrigerate for at least 2 hours, or overnight.

This allows the chia seeds to absorb the liquid and thicken.
5. After the pudding has set, give it a good stir to break up any clumps and ensure an even texture.
6. Divide the Almond Joy chia pudding into serving cups or bowls.
7. Optional: Top each serving with a sprinkle of dark chocolate chips for added indulgence.
8. Enjoy your delightful Almond Joy Chia Dream!

Notes:

- This pudding can be stored in the refrigerator for up to 5 days.
- For a thicker pudding, use less milk. For a thinner consistency, add more milk.
- You can toast the shredded coconut and sliced almonds before adding them for an extra layer of flavor.
- Adjust the sweetness to your liking by adding more or less maple syrup or honey.
- Feel free to get creative with toppings like additional sliced almonds or a drizzle of almond butter.

Pumpkin Spice Chia Harvest

Ingredients:

- 1/4 cup chia seeds
- 1 cup milk (almond milk, coconut milk, or any milk of your choice)
- 1/2 cup pumpkin puree
- 2 tablespoons maple syrup or honey (adjust to taste)
- 1/2 teaspoon pumpkin pie spice (or a mixture of cinnamon, nutmeg, and cloves)
- 1/2 teaspoon vanilla extract
- Optional toppings: whipped cream, chopped pecans, additional pumpkin pie spice

Instructions:

1. In a mixing bowl, combine the chia seeds, milk, pumpkin puree, maple syrup (or honey), pumpkin pie spice, and vanilla extract.
2. Whisk everything together until well combined and the pumpkin puree is evenly distributed.
3. Cover the bowl with plastic wrap or a lid and refrigerate for at least 2 hours, or overnight. This allows the chia seeds to absorb the liquid and thicken.

4. After the pudding has set, give it a good stir to break up any clumps and ensure an even texture.
5. Divide the Pumpkin Spice chia pudding into serving cups or bowls.
6. Optional: Top each serving with a dollop of whipped cream, chopped pecans, and a sprinkle of additional pumpkin pie spice.
7. Enjoy the warm flavors of fall with your Pumpkin Spice Chia Harvest!

Notes:

- This pudding can be stored in the refrigerator for up to 5 days.
- Adjust the sweetness to your liking by adding more or less maple syrup or honey.
- If you don't have pumpkin pie spice, you can make your own by mixing cinnamon, nutmeg, and cloves in equal parts.
- Feel free to experiment with toppings like caramel drizzle or a sprinkle of toasted coconut.

Matcha Green Tea Chia Zen

Ingredients:

- 1/4 cup chia seeds
- 1 cup milk (almond milk, coconut milk, or any milk of your choice)
- 1 tablespoon matcha green tea powder
- 2-3 tablespoons maple syrup or honey (adjust to taste)
- 1/2 teaspoon vanilla extract
- Optional toppings: sliced strawberries, kiwi, or a sprinkle of matcha powder

Instructions:

1. In a mixing bowl, combine the chia seeds, milk, matcha green tea powder, maple syrup (or honey), and vanilla extract.
2. Whisk everything together until the matcha powder is fully incorporated and there are no lumps.
3. Cover the bowl with plastic wrap or a lid and refrigerate for at least 2 hours, or overnight. This allows the chia seeds to absorb the liquid and thicken.
4. After the pudding has set, give it a good stir to break up any clumps and ensure an even texture.

5. Divide the Matcha Green Tea chia pudding into serving cups or bowls.
6. Optional: Top each serving with sliced strawberries, kiwi, or a sprinkle of matcha powder for extra flavor and presentation.
7. Enjoy your calming Matcha Green Tea Chia Zen!

Notes:

- This pudding can be stored in the refrigerator for up to 5 days.
- Adjust the sweetness to your liking by adding more or less maple syrup or honey.
- If you prefer a stronger matcha flavor, increase the amount of matcha powder.
- Experiment with different toppings such as mango, pineapple, or blueberries for variety.

Salted Caramel Chia Delight

Ingredients:

- 1/4 cup chia seeds
- 1 cup milk (almond milk, coconut milk, or any milk of your choice)
- 3 tablespoons caramel sauce (store-bought or homemade)
- 1/2 teaspoon vanilla extract
- 1/4 teaspoon sea salt (plus extra for garnish)
- Optional toppings: whipped cream, chopped pecans, additional caramel sauce

Instructions:

1. In a mixing bowl, combine the chia seeds, milk, caramel sauce, vanilla extract, and sea salt.
2. Whisk everything together until well combined.
3. Cover the bowl with plastic wrap or a lid and refrigerate for at least 2 hours, or overnight. This allows the chia seeds to absorb the liquid and thicken.
4. After the pudding has set, give it a good stir to break up any clumps and ensure an even texture.

5. Divide the Salted Caramel chia pudding into serving cups or bowls.
6. Optional: Top each serving with a dollop of whipped cream, chopped pecans, a drizzle of additional caramel sauce, and a sprinkle of sea salt.
7. Enjoy your decadent Salted Caramel Chia Delight!

Notes:

- This pudding can be stored in the refrigerator for up to 5 days.
- For a richer caramel flavor, you can use dulce de leche instead of caramel sauce.
- If you don't have caramel sauce, you can make a quick caramel by melting sugar in a saucepan until golden brown, then adding cream and butter.
- Adjust the sweetness and saltiness to your liking by adding more or less caramel sauce and sea salt.
- Feel free to get creative with toppings like chocolate shavings or a sprinkle of cinnamon.

Espresso Hazelnut Chia Euphoria

Ingredients:

- 1/4 cup chia seeds
- 1 cup milk (almond milk, coconut milk, or any milk of your choice)
- 1-2 shots of espresso (or 1/2 cup strong brewed coffee)
- 2 tablespoons hazelnut spread (such as Nutella)
- 2 tablespoons maple syrup or honey (adjust to taste)
- 1/2 teaspoon vanilla extract
- Optional toppings: whipped cream, chopped hazelnuts, chocolate shavings

Instructions:

1. In a mixing bowl, combine the chia seeds, milk, espresso (or coffee), hazelnut spread, maple syrup (or honey), and vanilla extract.
2. Whisk everything together until well combined.
3. Cover the bowl with plastic wrap or a lid and refrigerate for at least 2 hours, or overnight. This allows the chia seeds to absorb the liquid and thicken.

4. After the pudding has set, give it a good stir to break up any clumps and ensure an even texture.
5. Divide the Espresso Hazelnut chia pudding into serving cups or bowls.
6. Optional: Top each serving with a dollop of whipped cream, chopped hazelnuts, and chocolate shavings for an extra indulgent treat.
7. Enjoy your Espresso Hazelnut Chia Euphoria!

Notes:

- This pudding can be stored in the refrigerator for up to 5 days.
- If you don't have hazelnut spread, you can use hazelnut extract or finely chopped hazelnuts.
- Adjust the sweetness to your liking by adding more or less maple syrup or honey.
- For a stronger coffee flavor, add an extra shot of espresso or coffee.
- Feel free to get creative with toppings like a sprinkle of cocoa powder or a drizzle of caramel sauce.

Pomegranate Passion Chia Bliss

Ingredients:

- 1/4 cup chia seeds
- 1 cup pomegranate juice
- 1/2 cup coconut milk (or any milk of your choice)
- 2 tablespoons honey or maple syrup (adjust to taste)
- 1/2 teaspoon vanilla extract
- Optional toppings: pomegranate arils, sliced strawberries, mint leaves

Instructions:

1. In a mixing bowl, combine the chia seeds, pomegranate juice, coconut milk, honey (or maple syrup), and vanilla extract.
2. Whisk everything together until well combined.
3. Cover the bowl with plastic wrap or a lid and refrigerate for at least 2 hours, or overnight. This allows the chia seeds to absorb the liquid and thicken.
4. After the pudding has set, give it a good stir to break up any clumps and ensure an even texture.

5. Divide the Pomegranate Passion chia pudding into serving cups or bowls.
6. Optional: Top each serving with pomegranate arils, sliced strawberries, and mint leaves for freshness.
7. Enjoy the refreshing and nutritious Pomegranate Passion Chia Bliss!

Notes:

- This pudding can be stored in the refrigerator for up to 5 days.
- If you prefer a thicker pudding, use less coconut milk. For a thinner consistency, add more coconut milk.
- You can use fresh pomegranate juice or store-bought, just make sure it's 100% pure pomegranate juice.
- Adjust the sweetness to your liking by adding more or less honey or maple syrup.
- Feel free to get creative with toppings like granola, chopped nuts, or a drizzle of honey.

Lemon Raspberry Chia Symphony

Ingredients:

- 1/4 cup chia seeds
- 1 cup milk (almond milk, coconut milk, or any milk of your choice)
- Zest of 1 lemon
- 3 tablespoons fresh lemon juice
- 2-3 tablespoons maple syrup or honey (adjust to taste)
- 1/2 cup fresh raspberries
- Optional toppings: additional raspberries, lemon slices, mint leaves

Instructions:

1. In a mixing bowl, combine the chia seeds, milk, lemon zest, lemon juice, and maple syrup (or honey).
2. Whisk everything together until well combined.
3. Gently fold in the fresh raspberries, mashing some of them slightly to release their juices.
4. Cover the bowl with plastic wrap or a lid and refrigerate for at least 2 hours, or overnight. This allows the chia seeds to absorb the liquid and thicken.

5. After the pudding has set, give it a good stir to distribute the raspberries evenly.
6. Divide the Lemon Raspberry chia pudding into serving cups or bowls.
7. Optional: Top each serving with additional fresh raspberries, lemon slices, and mint leaves for a beautiful presentation.
8. Enjoy the refreshing and vibrant flavors of Lemon Raspberry Chia Symphony!

Notes:

- This pudding can be stored in the refrigerator for up to 5 days.
- Feel free to adjust the sweetness to your liking by adding more or less maple syrup or honey.
- If you prefer a smoother texture, you can blend the mixture (excluding raspberries) before refrigerating.
- For added lemon flavor, you can add a few drops of lemon extract.
- Experiment with different berries like blueberries or strawberries for variation.

Maple Walnut Chia Symphony

Ingredients:

- 1/4 cup chia seeds
- 1 cup milk (almond milk, coconut milk, or any milk of your choice)
- 3 tablespoons maple syrup
- 1/2 teaspoon vanilla extract
- 1/4 teaspoon ground cinnamon
- 1/4 cup chopped walnuts
- Optional toppings: additional maple syrup, extra chopped walnuts

Instructions:

1. In a mixing bowl, combine the chia seeds, milk, maple syrup, vanilla extract, and ground cinnamon.
2. Whisk everything together until well combined.
3. Gently fold in the chopped walnuts.
4. Cover the bowl with plastic wrap or a lid and refrigerate for at least 2 hours, or overnight. This allows the chia seeds to absorb the liquid and thicken.
5. After the pudding has set, give it a good stir to distribute the walnuts evenly.

6. Divide the Maple Walnut chia pudding into serving cups or bowls.
7. Optional: Drizzle each serving with additional maple syrup and sprinkle extra chopped walnuts on top.
8. Enjoy the delicious and nutritious Maple Walnut Chia Symphony!

Notes:

- This pudding can be stored in the refrigerator for up to 5 days.
- Adjust the sweetness to your liking by adding more or less maple syrup.
- You can toast the walnuts before adding them to the pudding for a deeper flavor.
- For added richness, you can use coconut milk instead of regular milk.
- Feel free to get creative with toppings like a sprinkle of nutmeg or a dollop of Greek yogurt.

Blueberry Lemon Cheesecake Chia Extravaganza

Ingredients:

- 1/4 cup chia seeds
- 1 cup milk (almond milk, coconut milk, or any milk of your choice)
- Zest of 1 lemon
- 3 tablespoons fresh lemon juice
- 2-3 tablespoons maple syrup or honey (adjust to taste)
- 1/2 teaspoon vanilla extract
- 1/4 cup cream cheese, softened
- 1/2 cup fresh blueberries
- Optional toppings: additional blueberries, lemon slices, mint leaves

Instructions:

1. In a mixing bowl, combine the chia seeds, milk, lemon zest, lemon juice, maple syrup (or honey), and vanilla extract.
2. Whisk everything together until well combined.
3. In a separate bowl, mix the softened cream cheese until smooth and creamy.
4. Slowly fold the cream cheese into the chia mixture until well incorporated.

5. Gently fold in the fresh blueberries.
6. Cover the bowl with plastic wrap or a lid and refrigerate for at least 2 hours, or overnight. This allows the chia seeds to absorb the liquid and thicken.
7. After the pudding has set, give it a good stir to distribute the blueberries and cream cheese.
8. Divide the Blueberry Lemon Cheesecake chia pudding into serving cups or bowls.
9. Optional: Top each serving with additional fresh blueberries, lemon slices, and mint leaves for a beautiful presentation.
10. Enjoy the delightful combination of flavors in your Blueberry Lemon Cheesecake Chia Extravaganza!

Notes:

- This pudding can be stored in the refrigerator for up to 5 days.
- Feel free to adjust the sweetness to your liking by adding more or less maple syrup or honey.
- If you prefer a smoother texture, you can blend the mixture (excluding blueberries) before refrigerating.
- For added texture, you can sprinkle crushed graham crackers on top before serving.
- Experiment with different berries like strawberries or raspberries for variation.

Peanut Butter Banana Chia Heaven

Ingredients:

- 1/4 cup chia seeds
- 1 cup milk (almond milk, coconut milk, or any milk of your choice)
- 2 tablespoons peanut butter (creamy or crunchy)
- 1-2 tablespoons maple syrup or honey (adjust to taste)
- 1 ripe banana, mashed
- 1/2 teaspoon vanilla extract
- Optional toppings: sliced bananas, a drizzle of peanut butter, chopped peanuts

Instructions:

1. In a mixing bowl, combine the chia seeds, milk, peanut butter, maple syrup (or honey), mashed banana, and vanilla extract.
2. Whisk everything together until well combined.
3. Cover the bowl with plastic wrap or a lid and refrigerate for at least 2 hours, or overnight. This allows the chia seeds to absorb the liquid and thicken.

4. After the pudding has set, give it a good stir to distribute the banana and peanut butter evenly.
5. Divide the Peanut Butter Banana chia pudding into serving cups or bowls.
6. Optional: Top each serving with sliced bananas, a drizzle of peanut butter, and chopped peanuts for added texture.
7. Enjoy your delicious Peanut Butter Banana Chia Heaven!

Notes:

- This pudding can be stored in the refrigerator for up to 5 days.
- Adjust the sweetness to your liking by adding more or less maple syrup or honey.
- If you prefer a smoother texture, you can blend the mixture (excluding bananas) before refrigerating.
- For added crunch, you can stir in some granola just before serving.
- Feel free to experiment with toppings like shredded coconut or a sprinkle of cinnamon.

Tiramisu Toffee Chia Temptation

Ingredients:

- 1/4 cup chia seeds
- 1 cup milk (almond milk, coconut milk, or any milk of your choice)
- 2 tablespoons instant coffee granules
- 2-3 tablespoons maple syrup or honey (adjust to taste)
- 1/2 teaspoon vanilla extract
- 1/4 cup toffee bits
- Optional toppings: whipped cream, cocoa powder, additional toffee bits

Instructions:

1. In a mixing bowl, combine the chia seeds, milk, instant coffee granules, maple syrup (or honey), and vanilla extract.
2. Whisk everything together until well combined.
3. Gently fold in the toffee bits.
4. Cover the bowl with plastic wrap or a lid and refrigerate for at least 2 hours, or overnight. This allows the chia seeds to absorb the liquid and thicken.

5. After the pudding has set, give it a good stir to distribute the toffee bits evenly.
6. Divide the Tiramisu Toffee chia pudding into serving cups or bowls.
7. Optional: Top each serving with a dollop of whipped cream, a sprinkle of cocoa powder, and additional toffee bits for a decadent touch.
8. Enjoy the rich flavors of Tiramisu Toffee Chia Temptation!

Notes:

- This pudding can be stored in the refrigerator for up to 5 days.
- Adjust the sweetness and coffee intensity to your liking by adding more or less maple syrup or honey, and instant coffee granules.
- If you prefer a smoother texture, you can blend the mixture (excluding toffee bits) before refrigerating.
- For added indulgence, you can layer the chia pudding with ladyfinger cookies soaked in coffee.
- Feel free to get creative with toppings like chocolate shavings or a drizzle of caramel sauce.

Pistachio Rosewater Chia Serenity

Ingredients:

- 1/4 cup chia seeds
- 1 cup milk (almond milk, coconut milk, or any milk of your choice)
- 2 tablespoons pistachios, finely chopped
- 2-3 tablespoons maple syrup or honey (adjust to taste)
- 1/2 teaspoon rosewater
- Optional toppings: chopped pistachios, edible rose petals

Instructions:

1. In a mixing bowl, combine the chia seeds, milk, chopped pistachios, maple syrup (or honey), and rosewater.
2. Whisk everything together until well combined.
3. Cover the bowl with plastic wrap or a lid and refrigerate for at least 2 hours, or overnight. This allows the chia seeds to absorb the liquid and thicken.
4. After the pudding has set, give it a good stir to distribute the pistachios and rosewater evenly.

5. Divide the Pistachio Rosewater chia pudding into serving cups or bowls.
6. Optional: Top each serving with additional chopped pistachios and edible rose petals for a beautiful presentation.
7. Enjoy the calming and aromatic Pistachio Rosewater Chia Serenity!

Notes:

- This pudding can be stored in the refrigerator for up to 5 days.
- If you prefer a smoother texture, you can blend the mixture (excluding pistachios) before refrigerating.
- Adjust the sweetness to your liking by adding more or less maple syrup or honey.
- For a more intense rose flavor, you can increase the amount of rosewater.
- Feel free to get creative with toppings like a sprinkle of cardamom or a drizzle of honey.

Orange Creamsicle Chia Fantasy

Ingredients:

- 1/4 cup chia seeds
- 1 cup milk (almond milk, coconut milk, or any milk of your choice)
- Zest of 1 orange
- 1/2 cup freshly squeezed orange juice
- 2-3 tablespoons maple syrup or honey (adjust to taste)
- 1/2 teaspoon vanilla extract
- Optional: 1/4 cup Greek yogurt or coconut yogurt for extra creaminess
- Optional toppings: orange slices, whipped cream, grated dark chocolate

Instructions:

1. In a mixing bowl, combine the chia seeds, milk, orange zest, orange juice, maple syrup (or honey), and vanilla extract.
2. If using, add the Greek yogurt or coconut yogurt for extra creaminess.
3. Whisk everything together until well combined.
4. Cover the bowl with plastic wrap or a lid and refrigerate for at least 2 hours, or overnight.

This allows the chia seeds to absorb the liquid and thicken.
5. After the pudding has set, give it a good stir to distribute the orange zest and yogurt evenly.
6. Divide the Orange Creamsicle chia pudding into serving cups or bowls.
7. Optional: Top each serving with orange slices, a dollop of whipped cream, and grated dark chocolate for an extra indulgent treat.
8. Enjoy the delightful and refreshing Orange Creamsicle Chia Fantasy!

Notes:

- This pudding can be stored in the refrigerator for up to 5 days.
- Adjust the sweetness to your liking by adding more or less maple syrup or honey.
- If you prefer a smoother texture, you can blend the mixture (excluding orange zest) before refrigerating.
- Feel free to add a pinch of cinnamon or nutmeg for extra flavor.
- For a dairy-free option, use coconut milk and coconut yogurt.

Strawberry Shortcake Chia Romance

Ingredients:

- 1/4 cup chia seeds
- 1 cup milk (almond milk, coconut milk, or any milk of your choice)
- 2 tablespoons maple syrup or honey (adjust to taste)
- 1/2 teaspoon vanilla extract
- 1 cup fresh strawberries, hulled and chopped
- 1 cup crumbled shortbread cookies
- Optional toppings: whipped cream, additional chopped strawberries, mint leaves

Instructions:

1. In a mixing bowl, combine the chia seeds, milk, maple syrup (or honey), and vanilla extract.
2. Whisk everything together until well combined.
3. Gently fold in the chopped strawberries.
4. Cover the bowl with plastic wrap or a lid and refrigerate for at least 2 hours, or overnight. This allows the chia seeds to absorb the liquid and thicken.

5. After the pudding has set, give it a good stir to distribute the strawberries evenly.
6. Layer the Strawberry Shortcake chia pudding and crumbled shortbread cookies in serving cups or bowls, starting with the pudding as the base.
7. Repeat the layers until you reach the top, finishing with a layer of crumbled shortbread cookies.
8. Optional: Top each serving with a dollop of whipped cream, additional chopped strawberries, and mint leaves for a beautiful presentation.
9. Enjoy the delightful Strawberry Shortcake Chia Romance!

Notes:

- This pudding can be stored in the refrigerator for up to 5 days.
- Adjust the sweetness to your liking by adding more or less maple syrup or honey.
- If you prefer a smoother texture, you can blend the mixture (excluding strawberries) before refrigerating.
- For a shortcut, you can use store-bought shortbread cookies instead of making them from scratch.

- Feel free to get creative with toppings like a sprinkle of cinnamon or a drizzle of chocolate sauce.

Chai Spiced Chia Latte Love

Ingredients:

- 1/4 cup chia seeds
- 1 cup milk (almond milk, coconut milk, or any milk of your choice)
- 2 teaspoons chai tea blend (or 2 chai tea bags)
- 2 tablespoons maple syrup or honey (adjust to taste)
- 1/2 teaspoon vanilla extract
- 1/4 teaspoon ground cinnamon
- 1/4 teaspoon ground ginger
- 1/8 teaspoon ground cardamom
- Pinch of ground cloves
- Pinch of ground nutmeg
- Optional toppings: whipped cream, cinnamon sticks, star anise

Instructions:

1. In a small saucepan, heat the milk over medium heat until steaming but not boiling.
2. If using chai tea bags, steep them in the hot milk for 5 minutes. If using chai tea blend, add it directly to the hot milk.
3. Remove the tea bags or strain out the chai tea blend from the milk using a fine-mesh sieve.

4. In a mixing bowl, combine the chia seeds, maple syrup (or honey), vanilla extract, ground cinnamon, ground ginger, ground cardamom, ground cloves, and ground nutmeg.
5. Gradually pour the warm chai-infused milk into the chia seed mixture, whisking continuously to prevent clumps.
6. Whisk until everything is well combined.
7. Cover the bowl with plastic wrap or a lid and refrigerate for at least 2 hours, or overnight. This allows the chia seeds to absorb the liquid and thicken.
8. After the pudding has set, give it a good stir to distribute the spices evenly.
9. Divide the Chai Spiced Chia Latte Love into serving cups or glasses.
10. Optional: Top each serving with a dollop of whipped cream, a sprinkle of ground cinnamon, and garnish with cinnamon sticks or star anise for a festive touch.
11. Enjoy the cozy and aromatic Chai Spiced Chia Latte Love!

Notes:

- This pudding can be stored in the refrigerator for up to 5 days.
- Adjust the sweetness to your liking by adding more or less maple syrup or honey.

- If you prefer a stronger chai flavor, you can increase the amount of chai tea blend or steep the tea longer.
- Feel free to get creative with toppings like a sprinkle of nutmeg or a drizzle of caramel sauce.

Cookies and Cream Chia Fantasy

Ingredients:

- 1/4 cup chia seeds
- 1 cup milk (almond milk, coconut milk, or any milk of your choice)
- 2 tablespoons cocoa powder
- 2 tablespoons maple syrup or honey (adjust to taste)
- 1/2 teaspoon vanilla extract
- 4-6 chocolate sandwich cookies, crushed (like Oreo cookies)
- Optional toppings: whipped cream, additional crushed cookies

Instructions:

1. In a mixing bowl, combine the chia seeds, milk, cocoa powder, maple syrup (or honey), and vanilla extract.
2. Whisk everything together until well combined.
3. Gently fold in the crushed chocolate sandwich cookies.
4. Cover the bowl with plastic wrap or a lid and refrigerate for at least 2 hours, or overnight.

This allows the chia seeds to absorb the liquid and thicken.
5. After the pudding has set, give it a good stir to distribute the cookies evenly.
6. Divide the Cookies and Cream chia pudding into serving cups or bowls.
7. Optional: Top each serving with a dollop of whipped cream and sprinkle with additional crushed cookies for extra crunch and sweetness.
8. Enjoy the delightful Cookies and Cream Chia Fantasy!

Notes:

- This pudding can be stored in the refrigerator for up to 5 days.
- Adjust the sweetness to your liking by adding more or less maple syrup or honey.
- You can use any chocolate sandwich cookies you prefer, such as Oreo cookies.
- For a richer flavor, you can use chocolate milk instead of regular milk.
- Feel free to get creative with toppings like a drizzle of chocolate sauce or a sprinkle of cocoa powder.

Cherry Almond Chia Jubilee

Ingredients:

- 1/4 cup chia seeds
- 1 cup milk (almond milk, coconut milk, or any milk of your choice)
- 2 tablespoons maple syrup or honey (adjust to taste)
- 1/2 teaspoon almond extract
- 1/2 cup fresh cherries, pitted and chopped
- 1/4 cup sliced almonds
- Optional toppings: additional fresh cherries, sliced almonds

Instructions:

1. In a mixing bowl, combine the chia seeds, milk, maple syrup (or honey), and almond extract.
2. Whisk everything together until well combined.
3. Gently fold in the chopped cherries and sliced almonds.
4. Cover the bowl with plastic wrap or a lid and refrigerate for at least 2 hours, or overnight. This allows the chia seeds to absorb the liquid and thicken.

5. After the pudding has set, give it a good stir to distribute the cherries and almonds evenly.
6. Divide the Cherry Almond chia pudding into serving cups or bowls.
7. Optional: Top each serving with additional fresh cherries and sliced almonds for a beautiful presentation.
8. Enjoy the delicious and nutritious Cherry Almond Chia Jubilee!

Notes:

- This pudding can be stored in the refrigerator for up to 5 days.
- Adjust the sweetness to your liking by adding more or less maple syrup or honey.
- If you prefer a smoother texture, you can blend the mixture (excluding cherries and almonds) before refrigerating.
- Feel free to experiment with different fruits like raspberries or blueberries.
- For added crunch, you can lightly toast the sliced almonds before adding them to the pudding.

Gingerbread Cookie Chia Joy

Ingredients:

- 1/4 cup chia seeds
- 1 cup milk (almond milk, coconut milk, or any milk of your choice)
- 2 tablespoons molasses
- 2 tablespoons maple syrup or honey (adjust to taste)
- 1/2 teaspoon ground ginger
- 1/2 teaspoon ground cinnamon
- 1/4 teaspoon ground nutmeg
- 1/4 teaspoon ground cloves
- 1/4 teaspoon vanilla extract
- 1/4 cup crumbled gingerbread cookies
- Optional toppings: whipped cream, additional crumbled gingerbread cookies, ground cinnamon

Instructions:

1. In a mixing bowl, combine the chia seeds, milk, molasses, maple syrup (or honey), ground ginger, ground cinnamon, ground nutmeg, ground cloves, and vanilla extract.
2. Whisk everything together until well combined.

3. Gently fold in the crumbled gingerbread cookies.
4. Cover the bowl with plastic wrap or a lid and refrigerate for at least 2 hours, or overnight. This allows the chia seeds to absorb the liquid and thicken.
5. After the pudding has set, give it a good stir to distribute the gingerbread cookies and spices evenly.
6. Divide the Gingerbread Cookie Chia Joy into serving cups or bowls.
7. Optional: Top each serving with a dollop of whipped cream, a sprinkle of additional crumbled gingerbread cookies, and a dusting of ground cinnamon for a festive touch.
8. Enjoy the cozy and festive Gingerbread Cookie Chia Joy!

Notes:

- This pudding can be stored in the refrigerator for up to 5 days.
- Adjust the sweetness to your liking by adding more or less maple syrup or honey.
- For a richer flavor, you can use a combination of milk and cream.
- If you prefer a smoother texture, you can blend the mixture (excluding gingerbread cookies) before refrigerating.

- Feel free to garnish with a sprinkle of chopped nuts or a drizzle of caramel sauce.

Chocolate Raspberry Chia Fantasy

Ingredients:

- 1/4 cup chia seeds
- 1 cup milk (almond milk, coconut milk, or any milk of your choice)
- 2 tablespoons cocoa powder
- 2 tablespoons maple syrup or honey (adjust to taste)
- 1/2 teaspoon vanilla extract
- 1/2 cup fresh raspberries
- Optional: 2 tablespoons chocolate chips
- Optional toppings: additional fresh raspberries, chocolate shavings

Instructions:

1. In a mixing bowl, combine the chia seeds, milk, cocoa powder, maple syrup (or honey), and vanilla extract.
2. Whisk everything together until well combined.
3. Gently fold in the fresh raspberries and chocolate chips (if using).
4. Cover the bowl with plastic wrap or a lid and refrigerate for at least 2 hours, or overnight.

This allows the chia seeds to absorb the liquid and thicken.
5. After the pudding has set, give it a good stir to distribute the raspberries and chocolate evenly.
6. Divide the Chocolate Raspberry chia pudding into serving cups or bowls.
7. Optional: Top each serving with additional fresh raspberries and chocolate shavings for a beautiful presentation.
8. Enjoy the decadent and fruity Chocolate Raspberry Chia Fantasy!

Notes:

- This pudding can be stored in the refrigerator for up to 5 days.
- Adjust the sweetness to your liking by adding more or less maple syrup or honey.
- If you prefer a smoother texture, you can blend the mixture (excluding raspberries and chocolate chips) before refrigerating.
- Feel free to substitute raspberries with strawberries or blackberries for variation.
- For a dairy-free option, use dairy-free chocolate chips.

Cinnamon Roll Chia Delight

Ingredients:

- 1/4 cup chia seeds
- 1 cup milk (almond milk, coconut milk, or any milk of your choice)
- 2 tablespoons maple syrup or honey (adjust to taste)
- 1/2 teaspoon vanilla extract
- 1/2 teaspoon ground cinnamon
- Pinch of ground nutmeg
- Pinch of salt
- 1/4 cup raisins
- 1/4 cup chopped pecans or walnuts
- Optional toppings: extra cinnamon, maple syrup, pecans or walnuts

Instructions:

1. In a mixing bowl, combine the chia seeds, milk, maple syrup (or honey), vanilla extract, ground cinnamon, ground nutmeg, and a pinch of salt.
2. Whisk everything together until well combined.
3. Gently fold in the raisins and chopped pecans or walnuts.

4. Cover the bowl with plastic wrap or a lid and refrigerate for at least 2 hours, or overnight. This allows the chia seeds to absorb the liquid and thicken.
5. After the pudding has set, give it a good stir to distribute the raisins and nuts evenly.
6. Divide the Cinnamon Roll Chia Delight into serving cups or bowls.
7. Optional: Top each serving with extra ground cinnamon, a drizzle of maple syrup, and a sprinkle of pecans or walnuts.
8. Enjoy the cozy and flavorful Cinnamon Roll Chia Delight!

Notes:

- This pudding can be stored in the refrigerator for up to 5 days.
- Adjust the sweetness to your liking by adding more or less maple syrup or honey.
- If you prefer a smoother texture, you can blend the mixture (excluding raisins and nuts) before refrigerating.
- Feel free to add a dash of vanilla extract for extra flavor.
- You can warm up the pudding slightly before serving for a comforting treat.

Hazelnut Honey Chia Harmony

Ingredients:

- 1/4 cup chia seeds
- 1 cup milk (almond milk, coconut milk, or any milk of your choice)
- 2 tablespoons hazelnut butter
- 2 tablespoons honey
- 1/2 teaspoon vanilla extract
- Pinch of salt
- Optional toppings: chopped hazelnuts, drizzle of honey

Instructions:

1. In a mixing bowl, combine the chia seeds, milk, hazelnut butter, honey, vanilla extract, and a pinch of salt.
2. Whisk everything together until well combined.
3. Cover the bowl with plastic wrap or a lid and refrigerate for at least 2 hours, or overnight. This allows the chia seeds to absorb the liquid and thicken.
4. After the pudding has set, give it a good stir to distribute the hazelnut butter and honey evenly.

5. Divide the Hazelnut Honey Chia Harmony into serving cups or bowls.
6. Optional: Top each serving with chopped hazelnuts and a drizzle of honey for an extra touch of sweetness and crunch.
7. Enjoy the delicious and nutty Hazelnut Honey Chia Harmony!

Notes:

- This pudding can be stored in the refrigerator for up to 5 days.
- You can substitute hazelnut butter with almond butter or any nut butter of your choice.
- Adjust the sweetness to your liking by adding more or less honey.
- If you prefer a smoother texture, you can blend the mixture (excluding chopped hazelnuts) before refrigerating.
- Feel free to experiment with different toppings like sliced bananas or a sprinkle of cinnamon.

Kiwi Lime Chia Zest

Ingredients:

- 1/4 cup chia seeds
- 1 cup coconut water (or water)
- 2 kiwi fruits, peeled and diced
- Zest of 1 lime
- 2 tablespoons honey or maple syrup (adjust to taste)
- Optional toppings: kiwi slices, lime slices, mint leaves

Instructions:

1. In a mixing bowl, combine the chia seeds and coconut water (or water).
2. Whisk everything together until well combined.
3. Add the diced kiwi fruits, lime zest, and honey or maple syrup to the chia mixture.
4. Stir gently to mix the ingredients.
5. Cover the bowl with plastic wrap or a lid and refrigerate for at least 2 hours, or overnight. This allows the chia seeds to absorb the liquid and thicken.
6. After the pudding has set, give it a good stir to distribute the kiwi and lime zest evenly.

7. Divide the Kiwi Lime Chia Zest into serving cups or bowls.
8. Optional: Top each serving with kiwi slices, lime slices, and mint leaves for a refreshing presentation.
9. Enjoy the vibrant and zesty Kiwi Lime Chia Zest!

Notes:

- This pudding can be stored in the refrigerator for up to 3-4 days.
- Adjust the sweetness to your liking by adding more or less honey or maple syrup.
- If you prefer a smoother texture, you can blend the mixture (excluding kiwi fruits and lime zest) before refrigerating.
- Feel free to add a squeeze of lime juice for extra tanginess.
- You can also experiment with other fruits like strawberries or pineapple.

Snickerdoodle Chia Celebration

Ingredients:

- 1/4 cup chia seeds
- 1 cup milk (almond milk, coconut milk, or any milk of your choice)
- 2 tablespoons maple syrup or honey (adjust to taste)
- 1/2 teaspoon vanilla extract
- 1/2 teaspoon ground cinnamon
- Pinch of salt
- For Coating:
- 2 tablespoons sugar
- 1 teaspoon ground cinnamon

Instructions:

1. In a mixing bowl, combine the chia seeds, milk, maple syrup (or honey), vanilla extract, ground cinnamon, and a pinch of salt.
2. Whisk everything together until well combined.
3. Cover the bowl with plastic wrap or a lid and refrigerate for at least 2 hours, or overnight. This allows the chia seeds to absorb the liquid and thicken.

4. After the pudding has set, prepare the coating by combining the sugar and ground cinnamon in a small bowl.
5. Using a small scoop or spoon, form the chilled chia pudding mixture into small balls and roll them in the cinnamon-sugar coating until evenly coated.
6. Place the coated chia balls on a plate or baking sheet lined with parchment paper.
7. Optional: Chill the Snickerdoodle Chia Celebration balls in the refrigerator for 30 minutes to firm up.
8. Enjoy these delightful Snickerdoodle Chia Celebration bites!

Notes:

- This recipe makes about 10-12 chia balls, depending on the size.
- Adjust the sweetness to your liking by adding more or less maple syrup or honey.
- If the chia mixture is too wet to roll into balls, add a little more chia seeds and let it sit for a few more minutes to thicken.
- You can also add a dash of ground nutmeg or allspice to the coating for extra flavor.
- Store the Snickerdoodle Chia Celebration balls in an airtight container in the refrigerator for up to 5 days.

Apple Pie Chia Extravaganza

Ingredients:

- 1/4 cup chia seeds
- 1 cup milk (almond milk, coconut milk, or any milk of your choice)
- 2 tablespoons maple syrup or honey (adjust to taste)
- 1/2 teaspoon vanilla extract
- 1/2 teaspoon ground cinnamon
- Pinch of ground nutmeg
- Pinch of ground cloves
- 1 large apple, peeled and finely chopped
- 1/4 cup chopped walnuts or pecans
- Optional toppings: whipped cream, additional chopped nuts, sprinkle of cinnamon

Instructions:

1. In a mixing bowl, combine the chia seeds, milk, maple syrup (or honey), vanilla extract, ground cinnamon, ground nutmeg, and ground cloves.
2. Whisk everything together until well combined.
3. Gently fold in the chopped apple and chopped nuts.

4. Cover the bowl with plastic wrap or a lid and refrigerate for at least 2 hours, or overnight. This allows the chia seeds to absorb the liquid and thicken.
5. After the pudding has set, give it a good stir to distribute the apples and nuts evenly.
6. Divide the Apple Pie Chia Extravaganza into serving cups or bowls.
7. Optional: Top each serving with a dollop of whipped cream, additional chopped nuts, and a sprinkle of cinnamon for a delightful apple pie flavor.
8. Enjoy the delicious and nutritious Apple Pie Chia Extravaganza!

Notes:

- This pudding can be stored in the refrigerator for up to 5 days.
- Adjust the sweetness to your liking by adding more or less maple syrup or honey.
- You can use any variety of apple you prefer, such as Granny Smith or Honeycrisp.
- Feel free to add a dash of lemon juice to the apples to prevent browning.
- For a crunchy texture, you can toast the chopped nuts before adding them to the pudding.

Lavender Blueberry Chia Serenade

Ingredients:

- 1/4 cup chia seeds
- 1 cup milk (almond milk, coconut milk, or any milk of your choice)
- 2 tablespoons honey or maple syrup (adjust to taste)
- 1/2 teaspoon vanilla extract
- 1/2 teaspoon dried culinary lavender flowers
- 1/2 cup fresh blueberries
- Optional toppings: additional fresh blueberries, lavender flowers

Instructions:

1. In a mixing bowl, combine the chia seeds, milk, honey (or maple syrup), vanilla extract, and dried lavender flowers.
2. Whisk everything together until well combined.
3. Gently fold in the fresh blueberries.
4. Cover the bowl with plastic wrap or a lid and refrigerate for at least 2 hours, or overnight. This allows the chia seeds to absorb the liquid and thicken.

5. After the pudding has set, give it a good stir to distribute the blueberries and lavender evenly.
6. Divide the Lavender Blueberry Chia Serenade into serving cups or bowls.
7. Optional: Top each serving with additional fresh blueberries and a sprinkle of lavender flowers for a beautiful presentation.
8. Enjoy the soothing and refreshing Lavender Blueberry Chia Serenade!

Notes:

- This pudding can be stored in the refrigerator for up to 5 days.
- Adjust the sweetness to your liking by adding more or less honey or maple syrup.
- If you don't have dried culinary lavender flowers, you can use lavender tea leaves or skip this ingredient.
- Feel free to experiment with other berries like raspberries or blackberries.
- For a creamier texture, you can use coconut cream instead of milk.

www.ingramcontent.com/pod-product-compliance
Lightning Source LLC
LaVergne TN
LVHW010224290125
802436LV00016B/154